Thor Heyerdahl

Across the Seas of Time

by Paul Westman

DILLON PRESS, INC. MINNEAPOLIS, MINNESOTA

Library of Congress Cataloging in Publication Data

Westman, Paul
  Thor Heyerdahl, across the seas of time.

  (Taking part)
  SUMMARY: A biography of the Norwegian explorer whose many
voyages were undertaken to prove certain theories about the migration
patterns of ancient people.
  1. Heyerdahl, Thor   —Juvenile literature.
  2. Explorers—Norway—Biography—Juvenile literature.
  [1. Heyerdahl, Thor.   2. Explorers] I. Title.
  G306.H47W47   910'.92'4 [B] [92]   82-1431
  ISBN 0-87518-225-9   AACR2

Dillon Press, Inc., 500 South Third Street
Minneapolis, Minnesota 55415

Printed in the United States of America

*The photographs are reproduced through
the courtesy of Thor Heyerdahl.
Back cover photograph by Walter Leonardi.*

THOR HEYERDAHL

Thor Heyerdahl, a world-renowned scientist, adventurer, and writer, grew up in the coastal town of Larvik, Norway. As a boy, Thor dreamed about traveling to the South Seas because life seemed so peaceful and simple there. A trip to the Polynesian island of Fatu Hiva in 1936 sparked his lifelong interest in the voyages of ancient peoples.

Heyerdahl crossed many oceans to show how the ancients sailed the seas. In 1947 he floated from Peru to Polynesia on a wooden raft called the *Kon-Tiki*. In 1955 he led an expedition to uncover the mystery of the giant stone statues that stand on Easter Island. Sixteen years later, he traveled from Morocco to the West Indies on the *Ra II*, a reed boat like those used by the ancient Egyptians. And in 1977 he sailed from Iraq to Pakistan to Africa in another reed ship, the *Tigris*, just as the ancient Sumerians had done.

These voyages across the seas of time made Heyerdahl famous. A number of scientific organizations honored his work; in addition, millions of people around the world read his books—*Kon-Tiki*, *Aku-Aku*, *The Ra Expeditions*, *The Tigris Expedition*. All of them agreed that he had successfully combined "a sense of adventure with a search for history."

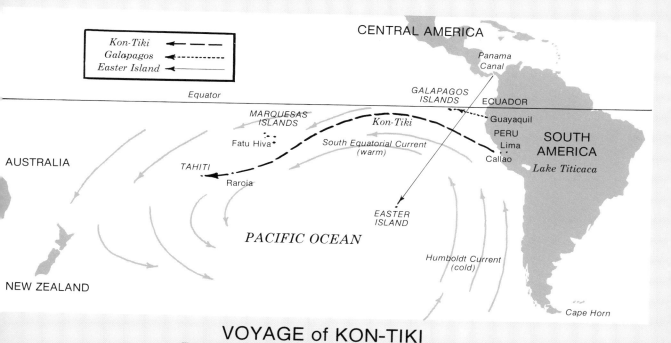

VOYAGE of KON-TIKI
Expeditions to the Galapagos and Easter Island

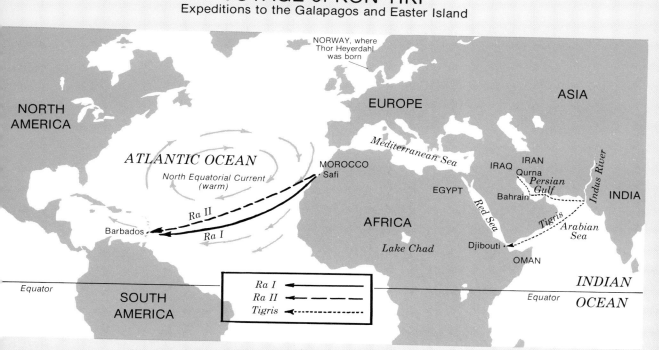

VOYAGES OF RA I, RA II, and the TIGRIS

Thor Heyerdahl, the brave sailor who crossed the Pacific Ocean on a wooden raft called the Kon-Tiki, *grew up in snowy Larvik, Norway.*

The sea came towering up again. The six men disappeared in a wall of green water.

The water rushed over them. It tore at their hands and bodies. But it was not as strong as before.

Now they had their chance. One by one they jumped onto the coral reef. The shallow bay and white beach of a tiny island lay before them. Gathering strength, they struggled to shore. Finally, they were safe. Their 4,300-mile trip across the Pacific Ocean on a wooden raft was over.

One of these six men was Thor Heyerdahl. He was their leader. Now 32 years old, he had once been deathly afraid of the ocean.

Thor Heyerdahl was born in Larvik, Norway, on October 6, 1914. He was named Thor after his father, a successful businessman. His mother Alison was in charge of the Larvik Museum. The family lived in a long wooden house on a hill above the town's harbor.

Both his parents had been married before, so Thor had several half-brothers. These brothers were much older than Thor, however, and they left home while he was still young.

Thor was a quiet boy who did not make friends easily. He was trimly built, with blue eyes and blond hair. Small and shy, he kept to himself.

Mr. Heyerdahl let Thor sit on the back of a small goat.

Thor and his mother stand on the steps of the family's tall wooden house in Larvik, Norway.

Often, he was lonely and wished he had a brother or sister.

Thor's mother was interested in wood carving, animals, and ancient peoples. Thor shared her interests, especially in animals. He knew the Latin names of even the rarest animals. Thor told his mother that he hoped to become a zoologist, a scientist who studies animals.

When he was seven, Thor started a collection. It was made up of snakes, shells, starfish, crabs, butterflies, and insects. Some of the best samples were given to him by his father, who brought them back from his business trips. Thor preserved his collection in jars of alcohol or in glass-topped boxes in his room.

After a time, Thor moved his collection to a former stable behind his family's house. He turned the stable into a little museum called Animal House. Children as well as grown-ups came to look at Thor's collection. One day several teachers brought their classes. This visit pleased Thor very much.

Mr. Heyerdahl and Thor went hiking in the fields and forests around Larvik. Often they followed animal tracks. Mr. Heyerdahl liked to hunt, but Thor did not. He did not enjoy shooting animals for sport.

On top of a hill near Thor's home was a pond. Years ago the pond had supplied water to a Danish count's manor house and fountains. That is why it was known as Manor Pond.

Thor often climbed the old moss-covered steps that led to Manor Pond. Then he would sit on the hill, look at the insects in the grass, and listen to the wind in the trees. This was one of his favorite places to be alone.

Thor also liked to read. Many of the books he read were about animals, but some were about people who lived in faraway places. One of his favorite books showed pictures of people from Polynesia sitting in wooden canoes. Polynesia is a group of islands in the South Pacific Ocean.

One day Thor was playing with some friends. He became careless and fell into the sea. He went under the water twice before his friends saved him. For years afterward, Thor was afraid of the sea.

In 1928 Thor entered Larvik Middle School. In America, the middle school would have been called a junior high. Thor soon became bored with school. Instead of doing his work, he dreamed about faraway lands.

Many boys who were Thor's age began to play football and to run races. Thor did not care for sports. Although he became a good athlete, he was not interested in winning games or races.

Thor became one of the best cross-country skiers in Larvik. But when he felt like taking a rest in the middle of a race, he took it. Once he left a race to follow some animal tracks he had seen. For these reasons, he usually came in last.

Thor spent his vacations from school at his parents' cabin at Hörnsjö, a lake 150 miles from Oslo. Hörnsjö was high in the mountains. It was surrounded by thick forests and mountain meadows. The lake was sparkling clear and very cold.

(Top) In wintertime Thor explored the Norwegian mountains on skis. (Bottom) Thor and his dog Kazan rest in front of an igloo he built for shelter while traveling in the mountains.

Jagged peaks nearby were covered with snow most of the year.

Thor explored the hills and valleys around Hörnsjö until he knew them by heart. During winter vacations he traveled by dogsled or on skis. In summer he went on foot.

One day Thor and his mother took a long hike in the mountains. They came across a tumble-down cabin that belonged to a mountain man named Ola Björneby. Ola made his living by hunting and fishing.

Later, Thor and Ola became friends. One summer vacation, Thor stayed with the mountain man. Ola taught Thor how to hunt and fish using simple tools, how to read signs, and how to find his way when he was lost.

After graduating from the Larvik Gymnasium, or high school, in 1933, Thor entered the University of Oslo. Oslo is a seaport and the capital of Norway. The University of Oslo is the largest in the country.

In college Thor continued to study animals. He

also went on long hikes in the mountains. Often his friend, Erik Hesselberg, or his cousin, Gunnar Nissen, went with him. Several times the men were stranded by snowstorms. Thor wrote articles about these adventures and sold them to Norwegian newspapers.

In addition to learning more about animals, Thor studied geography. He read everything he could find dealing with tropical regions. One area he became interested in was the Marquesas Islands. They were part of the Polynesian islands he had wanted to travel to as a boy. Owned by France, the Marquesas Islands are 2,000 miles southeast of Hawaii.

Thor learned everything he could about Polynesia. He met an Oslo businessman who had lived in Tahiti, another Polynesian island. The businessman owned the world's largest private collection of books and maps on Polynesia. He allowed Thor to use them whenever he wished.

Thor began planning a trip to Polynesia while he was still in college. He asked his teachers to help him find a special study to do on one of the Polynesian islands. Then he told his father about his plans, and Mr. Heyerdahl agreed to pay for the trip. He thought Thor only wanted to carry out a scientific study.

But Thor really wanted to live in Polynesia. Life in Polynesia was peaceful and simple. The weather there was warm and sunny. Most important, Polynesia had no cars, telephones, offices, or factories. Thor was sick of these modern inventions. He wanted to live without them, just as Ola Björneby had done. "I was the world's first hippie," he joked years later.

Then Thor met a girl named Liv Torp, a student at the university. She liked Thor's idea of living a simple life without modern inventions. She also liked Thor. On Christmas Eve 1936, they were married. In January of 1937 they left Norway for the island of Fatu Hiva.

First the Heyerdahls journeyed to Tahiti. In Tahiti Thor and Liv made friends with a Polynesian chief, Teriieroo. He taught Thor and Liv how to live in the jungle, how to find food, and how to bake tropical dishes.

One day the chief invited Thor and Liv to a feast. At the feast the chief made Thor part of his family, naming him Terai Mateata. In Polynesian this meant "Blue Sky."

Finally a ship arrived to take Thor and Liv to Fatu Hiva. They boarded it and waved good-bye to Chief Teriieroo and their Polynesian friends. After the boat set sail, Liv and Thor saw nothing but ocean, flying fish, and whales for three weeks.

At last the Marquesas came into view. The islands were mountain tops rising out of the sea. Thor said that these mountains "hurled themselves ever higher as we sailed on. . . . Tumbling, frothing, rumbling like a distant thunderstorm, the endless sea beat wildly against [them]. . . . We seemed to be approaching ruins of a seagirt castle, with wisps of cloud sailing around the towers like smoke."

When they came to Fatu Hiva, the Heyerdahls put to shore in a small boat. A group of brown-skinned people was waiting for them on the beach. These people stared at the two newcomers, pointing and whispering. They had never seen a woman with such white skin as Liv's.

Finally one of the women in the group walked up to Liv, rubbed her finger against Liv's cheek, and burst out laughing. She thought Liv was wearing white make-up. Instead, she found that Liv's skin was really colored white!

Once on Fatu Hiva, the Heyerdahls built a bamboo hut beneath a high mountain. The roof was made of thatched palm leaves. Since the hut was close to the forest, Liv and Thor found coconuts, banana plants, sugar cane, oranges, and lemons to eat. These fruits and vegetables, along with fish, made up their diet.

Liv and Thor soon became friends with the people on Fatu Hiva. These people told many stories about their ancestors. They also showed Liv and Thor many ancient graves and stone carvings. Thor became so interested that he collected many old human skulls from the graves.

The mountains on Fatu Hiva tower over Liv and Thor's small bamboo hut (bottom center).

He also bought some small stone carvings from the islanders. One of the islanders sold him a robe made of human hair. It had been worn by one of the ancient rulers.

Thor learned as much as he could about the people who had once ruled the Marquesas. These people had come to the islands before history books were written. One question kept bothering Thor, though. How did the first settlers get there?

To the west of the Marquesas Islands is Asia. To the east is South America. Most scientists believed the settlers had come from Asia, since many islands are scattered between Asia and the Marquesas. But between the Marquesas and South America, there is nothing but water.

One of Thor's friends on Fatu Hiva was an old chief named Tei Tetua. Once he had been the ruler of four tribes. Now all his people were dead.

One night Thor sat with Tei Tetua before a fire on the beach. Waves crashed against the shore. Clouds drifted across the moon.

"The great chief Tiki brought my ancestors to

this island long ago," Tei Tetua said. "Before that, my people lived in a great land to the east, beyond the sea."

That night Thor thought about the old man's words. He listened to the waves beating against the shore. Suddenly he sat up. The waves on Fatu Hiva, he realized, always came from the east, as did the wind and the clouds.

Tei Tetua said his people had come from the east. Could the old man be right and the scientists wrong?

Thor and Liv returned to Norway in 1938. Thor was no longer interested in studying animals. From now on he would spend his life studying ancient peoples. Most of all, he wanted to learn more about the ancient Polynesians.

For 18 months, Thor did research in libraries and museums. He learned all he could about the Polynesians' history and way of life. The Polynesians, he finally decided, came from two different groups of settlers. The first settlers had come east to Polynesia from Peru. A second group of settlers had come from as far north as British Columbia, on the coast of Canada.

To test his ideas, Thor spent a year in British Columbia. There he studied and dug for ancient tools, dishes, and weapons. What he found made him certain of his ideas. Kwakiutl Indians from British Columbia had indeed settled Polynesia in ancient times.

But Thor was more interested in Polynesia's first settlers. This group was living in Polynesia before the Kwakiutl Indians arrived.

These earlier people were from Peru, in South America. Light-skinned and red-haired, they were said to have been a ruling class long before the time of the Incas. They built temples, cities, roads, and statues. They worshiped a sun god named Kon.

According to an old story, the light-skinned race had been wiped out in a great battle, about 500 A.D. The battle took place on the shores of Lake Titicaca, in the Andes Mountains. The tribe's leader, a chief named Kon-Tiki, escaped.

With some followers he went down to the Pacific and sailed out to sea.

This story reminded Thor of Tei Tetua's tale about a chief named Tiki. He wondered if this chief had sailed from Peru to Polynesia.

Thor also read reports written by the white sailors who later discovered Polynesia. These reports said that the first sailors found two types of people living on the islands. One type had black, coarse hair, brown skin, and black eyes. The other type had wavy, reddish-blond hair, light skin, and blue eyes.

The light-skinned people were called *urukehu*, and were said to be descendants of the first chiefs. By 1940 most of the *urukehu* were dead. Disease had killed them.

The sailors' reports puzzled Thor. Could the *urukehu* have been descendants of Kon-Tiki and his band?

Before he could find out, Norway was attacked by the German Nazis on April 9, 1940. Thor was in Canada at the time. Soon after, the Nazis took over Norway completely. The Norwegian king fled to London, England.

Norwegians who escaped the Nazis formed the Free Norwegian Army to win back their country. Inside Norway people established the Home Front to fight the Germans. Members of the Home Front spied on the Nazis and destroyed bridges, buildings, and weapons.

Thor could not ignore Norway's plight. He enlisted in the Free Norwegian Army and was sent to radio school in Little Norway, Canada.

Thor shows his son Björn a training camp for Norwegian soldiers near Toronto, Canada.

Lieutenant Heyerdahl (center) stands with two other Norwegian soldiers who fought the Germans in Finnmark.

Later he was sent to Scotland for advanced training.

After two years of training, Thor fought the Germans in Finnmark. Finnmark is above the Arctic Circle, in the northernmost part of Norway. Now a lieutenant, Thor led small bands of soldiers in hit and run attacks against the German army.

In 1945 the Germans were driven out of Norway. With his country free, Thor began to think about the first Polynesian settlers again. He did more research and more studying. At last he was sure his ideas were correct. The earliest Polynesians, led by Kon-Tiki, had indeed come from Peru.

Thor wrote a paper about his ideas and the results of his research. In 1946 he brought the paper to New York. But Thor was disappointed. Scientists scoffed at his ideas. No one would even read his paper, much less publish it.

One expert on Polynesia worked for a large museum in New York. Thor went to see him about the research paper.

The man had not read Thor's paper. He would not listen to Thor's ideas. "Nobody from South America ever reached the Pacific islands," he said sharply. "Do you know why?"

"Why?" Thor asked.

"Because they had no boats!"

"They had wooden rafts," Thor replied.

The scientist smiled. "Well, you can try to get from Peru to the Pacific islands on a wooden raft," he said.

Thor did not know what to say. He was certain

that it was possible to cross the ocean on a raft. But no one believed him. What could he do?

That evening Thor came to a decision. There was only one way to prove that he was right. He must cross the ocean on a raft.

Again the scientists scoffed. A wooden raft would break apart, they said. With only a square sail and one oar, it could not be steered. Besides, the distance between Peru and Polynesia was twice as far as even Columbus had sailed.

Thor went right on with his plans. He chose five crewmen to join him. Two of them, Torstein Raaby and Knut Haugland, were wartime friends. Another was his boyhood chum Erik Hesselberg. The other two were his new friends, Herman Watzinger and Bengt Danielsson. Only Hesselberg knew how to sail.

In the South American jungle, the men cut down nine giant trees. They lashed the trees together to make a raft, using no nails, pegs, or wire. According to explorers' diaries and old records, this was the way the raft should be built.

The men named it *Kon-Tiki* in honor of the great chief.

In the Pacific Ocean, the trade winds blow from east to west. Strong currents in the ocean flow in the same direction. They are like rivers in the larger sea. Thor relied on two of these currents, the Humboldt Current and the South Equatorial Current, to take the raft to Polynesia.

The men launched the *Kon-Tiki* on April 28, 1947. The Humboldt Current pulled them out to sea. Now there was no turning back. The raft could not be steered. It would float wherever the ocean took it.

The *Kon-Tiki* was at sea for 101 days. Waves crashed over the deck, but the water ran down between the logs. Sometimes the crew went swimming in the sea. Sometimes they rested in the bamboo hut on deck.

The men had brought their own food. But Thor wanted to know if ancient sailors could have fed themselves at sea. He found that the sea would have given them plenty to eat. His crew caught

On board the Kon-Tiki, *Knut Haugland (left),
Torstein Raaby (center), and Bengt Danielsson
(right) look at one day's catch of fish.*

fish by the dozens: dolphin fish, flying fish,
bonito, tuna, and even sharks. Edible seaweed
grew on the *Kon-Tiki*'s sides like plants in a
garden. Water was collected on the deck when it
rained.

Day after day, the *Kon-Tiki* moved westward. Most days it traveled about 42 miles. It sailed through gales, schools of sharks, and herds of whales. The whales could have splintered the little raft with a single blow of their mighty tails. But they left the men alone.

At last the crew arrived at a tiny island behind Raroia reef, south of the Marquesas Islands. No one lived on the palm-clad coral island, which had a white, shiny beach and a bay as smooth as blue glass. To the men, it looked like paradise.

The crew had to struggle to get to the island. But when they were all safely ashore, Thor knew he had proved his point: ancient peoples could have traveled to Polynesia by raft.

People from a nearby island came to help the men. Later a small French ship towed the raft to Tahiti. There Thor and the crew of the *Kon-Tiki* received a royal welcome. The whole island turned out to greet them. Thor's old friend, Chief Teriieroo, said, "Now we know where our fathers came from."

Near the end of their long voyage, the sight of the Polynesian islands cheered the crew of the Kon-Tiki.

When Thor returned to Norway, he had to pay back the money he had borrowed for the trip. To earn the money, he gave talks about the *Kon-Tiki* in Norway and the United States.

Thor did not make much money from giving these talks. His travels only tired him out and kept him away from his family. In fact, he and Liv saw so little of each other that they gradually grew apart. Later, they were divorced. Their two children, Thor, Jr., and Björn, stayed with Liv.

Afterward, Thor wrote a book called *Kon-Tiki* about the voyage. It was bought by millions of people around the world and was translated into 65 languages. A film Thor made, also called *Kon-Tiki*, won an Academy Award in 1951.

With the money from these projects, Thor led a group of scientists to the Galapagos Islands. These islands are also in the Pacific Ocean, about 700 miles west of Ecuador.

Thor studied several ancient camping places in the Galapagos. He found that coastal Indians from Ecuador and Peru had visited the islands

1,500 years before. This surprised many scientists. They thought that the islands had been discovered by Europeans more than a thousand years later.

In 1955 Thor led some scientists to Easter Island. It is 2,000 miles west of Chile. Huge statues, cut from solid blocks of stone, stand on the island's hillsides. Some weigh as much as 50 tons. These carvings puzzled scientists. Who could have made them?

Thor discovered many interesting facts about Easter Island. Two different groups, the "Long-ears" and "Short-ears," had settled there. The huge statues were carved by the Long-ears, a light-skinned, red-haired people.

Some of the islanders claimed to be descendants of the Long-ears. They showed Thor how their ancestors had cut and moved the stones. Their ancestors, they said, had been killed in a great battle 300 years before.

Thor wrote a book, *Aku-Aku*, about his Easter Island discoveries. Like *Kon-Tiki*, it was a best-

(Top) Huge, grim-faced statues, cut from solid blocks of stone, stand on Easter Island's hillsides. (Bottom) Descendants of the Long-ears show how their ancestors put up the huge statues.

seller. Aku-Aku is the islanders' name for "spirits."

Now world-famous, Thor returned to his 250-year-old house in Oslo. He was welcomed home by Yvonne, his second wife, and their daughter, Anette. Yvonne and Thor had been married in 1949, shortly after his divorce from Liv.

About a year after Thor came home, Yvonne gave birth to another girl, Marian. Thor did not have much time to enjoy the new baby, though. He became very ill with the flu and could not play with his children or do any work.

In 1958 the family moved to the Italian village of Colla Micheri. Thor thought the village would be a restful place to live, work, and bring up children. His third daughter, Bettina, was born there.

The family's house in Colla Micheri had no TV or telephones. The famous explorer did not even drive a car. Ever since his college days, he had not liked modern inventions.

For more than ten years Thor lived quietly. He

wrote, gave talks, and did research. At the same time, an idea was forming in his mind.

Both on Easter Island and on Lake Titicaca in Peru, Thor had seen boats made of reeds. The reeds used were like flower stalks. Making reed boats was an ancient art in South America.

Reed boats were also common in Mexico and Egypt. In addition, many other Egyptian and ancient South American Indian customs were alike. Picture writing, pyramids, mummies, calendars, and sun worship were some of them. Did ancient Egyptians or other early peoples sail reed boats to South America, bringing their customs with them? Thor decided to find out.

Once again scientists scoffed. A reed boat, they said, would break apart in salt water. One scientist even tested stalks of reed in a laboratory tank. They sank within two weeks.

Thor only smiled. "Test a piece of iron and you'd think an iron ship couldn't float," he said. "But it does. I'm putting my faith in the ancient peoples, just as I did with *Kon-Tiki*."

The *Ra*, Thor's reed boat, was designed from paintings and models of boats found in Egyptian tombs. Craftsmen from Lake Chad in central Africa built it. The builders knew nothing about the ocean. One of them, Abdullah, who later joined Thor's crew, did not even know the sea was salty.

"I load my vessels with people who know

Craftsmen from Lake Chad build the reed boat Ra I behind the Egyptian pyramids.

nothing about the sea," Thor said. "I want to show that crossing the ocean is not as hard as some people think."

The *Ra* set sail from Safi, Morocco, on May 25, 1969. It had a crew of seven: a Russian, an African from Chad, an American, an Italian, an Egyptian, a Mexican, and Thor, a Norwegian.

The Atlantic Ocean was stormy. Fierce waves

The Ra I *heads west from Morocco across the Atlantic Ocean.*

battered the little ship. After two months and 2,600 miles, the bundled reeds broke apart in a squall when their rope lashings snapped. The men swam under the boat to make repairs. Soon sharks were circling the boat. Because of the sharks, the men could no longer go into the water. Finally they had to leave the *Ra*. A small boat picked them up and took them to safety.

The crew of the Ra I *prepare to abandon their storm-battered ship.*

Still, Thor was not discouraged. He had sailed almost all the way from Africa to the West Indies in a reed boat other scientists said would sink. Certain of success, he began planning a second voyage.

His new ship, *Ra II*, was built by Aymara Indians from Lake Titicaca. It was smaller, lighter, and better made than *Ra I*. The ship carried the same food as early Egyptian sailors had taken: hard bread, nuts, honey, dates, cages of live poultry, and goatskins filled with water.

On May 17, 1970, *Ra II* set sail from Safi, Morocco. Two months later it came ashore at Barbados in the West Indies. Cheering people, 25,000 in all, greeted the brave crew. Another of Thor's ideas about ancient people crossing the ocean had proved correct.

The story of Thor's two adventures was told in *The Ra Expeditions*. The book showed that Thor was upset by the pollution he saw on the *Ra* voyages. When he had sailed on the *Kon-Tiki* just 23 years before, the water had been crystal clear.

This time it was often covered with spilled oil.

"The ocean cannot absorb all the chemical waste we dump into it," Thor said. He knew that life in the ocean was dying. If it died, life on the earth would soon die, too.

Thor made speeches and wrote articles to fight pollution. He also talked to special groups studying the problem. Eventually he became a pollution expert for the United Nations.

In 1972 Heyerdahl visited Iraq. There he studied another ancient people, the Sumerians. Around 3,000 B.C, the Sumerians had lived where the Tigris and Euphrates rivers meet. The Sumerians were the world's first great farmers, builders, traders, and soldiers.

Thor became interested in Sumerian shipping. He carefully studied old papers, books, drawings, and records. Soon he knew almost as much as an ancient Sumerian sea captain. "The Sumerians were master builders of reed ships," Thor said. "By ship, they probably had contacts with the earliest civilizations both in India and Africa."

Most historians did not share this view. They did not think of the Sumerians as sailors. Thor decided to correct their thinking.

He had a reed ship, the *Tigris*, built in Qurna, Iraq. Marsh Arabs from Iraq and Aymara Indians from Peru tied 33 tons of reeds into two long rolls. The rolls were lashed together with hemp to form the boat's hull. At the ends, the hull curled up like the toe of a genie's slipper.

The *Kon-Tiki* and the *Ra* had drifted with the westbound ocean currents. But in the Persian Gulf and the Arabian Sea, where Thor wanted to sail, there were no such currents. Thus, the builders made sure that the *Tigris* could be steered.

The *Tigris* was launched near Qurna, Iraq, on November 11, 1977. Once again the crew members came from countries all over the world. One person thought they were foolish to sail in a reed ship, calling them "eleven madmen in a fruit basket."

The ship sailed southeast down the Tigris

(Top) Aymara Indians from Peru and Marsh Arabs from Iraq used 33 tons of reeds to build the Tigris. (Bottom) Like an ancient Sumerian trading ship, the Tigris sailed from Iraq to Pakistan to Djibouti.

River to the Persian Gulf. Then it went east across the Arabian Sea to the mouth of the Indus River in Pakistan. From there it traveled southwest through the Arabian Sea and the Indian Ocean. Five months later, it sailed into the harbor of Djibouti, on the east coast of Africa.

Along the way, the *Tigris* docked at ancient trading ports. Here the Sumerians had traded copper, ivory, grain, and beads.

The *Tigris* constantly dodged huge oil tankers. In the night one of the tankers could easily run over the little boat. Since the *Tigris* was made of reeds, it did not show up on radar screens. One time a tanker came so close that the crew felt the heat of its engines.

During the voyage, Thor was shocked by the pollution he saw. In midocean the *Tigris* sailed into a band of orange waste. It sailed alongside the waste for a whole day, but the band had no beginning and no end.

The *Tigris* flew the flag of the United Nations. It sailed in peace. Yet every country in Africa

Thor looks at a slick band of orange waste polluting the Indian Ocean.

save one, Djibouti, refused to let it dock in their land. They were all at war.

Thor and his crew hated to see this fighting. They thought people should work together to solve the world's problems. To protest the fighting and the world trade in weapons, they burned the *Tigris* in Djibouti's harbor. Watching the ship go up in flames brought their voyage to a sad end.

A National Geographic TV special was made about the voyage of the *Tigris*. In addition, Thor wrote a book, *The Tigris Expedition*, about his trip.

Thor returned to Colla Micheri after sailing on the *Tigris*. He had always been happy there. Yet his house seemed empty now that his three daughters had grown up and left home. Anette had become an airline hostess, Marian a pottery maker, and Bettina a language student.

The house seemed even more empty when his wife Yvonne left. Several years after his return, she and Thor were divorced. She moved to Oslo, while he stayed in Colla Micheri.

Thor Heyerdahl is now 67 years old. He has spent his life working toward a single goal. This is to show that oceans have not kept people apart, as many scientists believe. Instead, oceans have helped to bring people together.

Recently, a reporter visited Thor in Italy. He and Thor talked for a long time. Finally the reporter asked, "Are you an adventurer?" Some scientists had called Thor that. They meant it as an insult.

Thor's blue eyes twinkled. "I'm not an adventurer," he said. "But I don't turn adventure down when it comes my way."

The Author

Paul Westman is a regular contributor to *Current Biography* and has written many books for young people, including several for the Taking Part series. Of the series, Westman says, "Young readers will learn something about well-known contemporary men and women in many challenging fields and at the same time begin to discover some of the joys of reading."

A recent graduate of the University of Minnesota, Westman lives in Minneapolis.